THE
PAPERCRAFT
IDEAS
BOOK

An Hachette UK Company
www.hachette.co.uk

First published in the United Kingdom in 2020 by
ILEX, an imprint of Octopus Publishing Group Ltd
Octopus Publishing Group
Carmelite House
50 Victoria Embankment
London, EC4Y 0DZ
www.octopusbooks.co.uk
www.octopusbooksusa.com

Design and layout copyright
© Octopus Publishing Group 2020
Text copyright © Jessica Baldry 2020

Front cover image © Molly McGrath
Back cover image © Sarah Louise Matthews

Distributed in the US by Hachette Book Group
1290 Avenue of the Americas
4th and 5th Floors New York, NY 10104

Distributed in Canada by Canadian Manda Group
664 Annette St., Toronto, Ontario Canada M6S 2C8

Publisher: Alison Starling
Editorial Director: Zena Alkayat
Commissioning Editor: Ellie Corbett
Managing Editor: Rachel Silverlight
Junior Editor: Stephanie Hetherington
Editorial Assistant: Ellen Sandford O'Neill
Art Director: Ben Gardiner
Designer: JC Lanaway
Picture Research: Jennifer Veall
Production Manager: Caroline Alberti

Jessica Baldry asserts the moral right to be
identified as the author of this work.

ISBN 978-1-78157-744-8

A CIP catalogue record for this book is available
from the British Library.

Printed and bound in China

10 9 8 7 6 5 4 3 2

THE PAPERCRAFT IDEAS BOOK

Jessica Baldry

ilex

Contents

Introduction 6–7

Everyday Life 8–9

3D Collage 10–11

Letterpress 12–13

Self Expression 14–15

Exploring Texture 16–17

Forests 18–19

Lighting 20–21

Vintage Papers 22–23

Decoration 24–25

People 26–27

Abstract Collage 28–29

Flowers 30–31

Mixing Papercraft with Illustration 32–33

Entomology 34–35

Exploring Pattern 36–37

Traditional Papercutting 38–39

Paper Quilling 40–41

Responding to a Brief 42–43

Cultural Heritage 44–45

Geometric Sculpture 46–47

Female Empowerment 48–49

Miniature 3D Sculptures 50–51

Cities and Landmarks 52–53

Working with Layers 54–55

Combining Digital with Handmade 56–57

Specialist Papers 58–59

Using Paper Stencils 60–61

Using Pattern Designs for Products 62–63

Paper Embossing 64–65

Hand-printed Wallpaper 66–67

Satellite Imagery 68–69

Bookmaking 70–71

Floral Patterns 72–73

Editorial Illustration 74–75

Paper Relief 76–77

Dreams and Inner Worlds 78–79

Repetition 80–81

Character Art 82–83

Photographing a 3D Paper Scene 84–85

Storytelling 86–87

Paper Marbling 88–89

Paper Engineering 90–91

Contemporary Papercutting 92–93

Wildlife 94–95

Collograph Printmaking 96–97

Paper and Thread 98–99

Architecture 100–101

Papercut Lightboxes 102–103

Nature's Beauty 104–105
Small-scale Collage 106–107
Personal Experiences
    and Identity 108–109
Craftsmanship vs
    Machine Precision 110–111
Papier Mâché 112–113
Greetings Cards 114–115
Block Printing onto Paper 116–117
Intricate Details 118–119
Origami 120–121
Hand Lettering 122–123
Mark-making 124–125
Iconic Buildings 126–127
Handmade Paper 128–129
Textiles 130–131
Jewellery 132–133
Paper Clay Forms 134–135
Visual Communication 136–137
Modelling with Paper 138–139
Dioramas 140–141
From Paper to Textiles 142–143
Paper Costume 144–145
Freehand Papercuts 146–147
Large-scale Sculpture 148–149
Printmaking with Stencils 150–151

Folk Art 152–153
Surrealism 154–155
Light and Shadow 156–157
Stop-motion Animation 158–159
Geometric Shapes 160–161
Cinema...................................... 162–163
Artist's Perspective 164–165
Sketching with Paper 166–167

Artist Credits 168–174
Author Biography.............................. 175
Acknowledgements
    and Picture Credits 176

Introduction

This book is a celebration of paper; a humble, yet incredibly versatile material that has been used both for creative and practical purposes over many centuries. It aims to explore the infinite ways paper can be crafted and manipulated to help you realize ideas and create stunning works of art. Papercraft is a broad area and encompasses a variety of techniques including traditional papercutting, quilling, sculpting and collage.

Many contemporary artists are drawn to paper for its simplicity, and challenge themselves to work creatively with both its limitations and strengths as a material. Some of the most talented artists and designers working with paper today have shared their processes and techniques in this book. The pages are filled with beautiful images, inspirational ideas and suggestions. Use these works as inspiration in order to explore the magical work of papercraft further within your own projects.

OPPOSITE:
A selection of Jessica
Baldry's papercuts

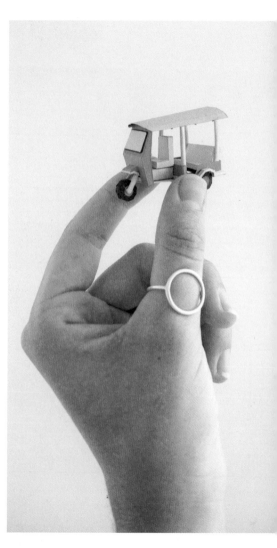

Everyday Life

INSPIRATION #1

—

Amy Mathers, based in Ireland, creates miniature paper sculptures of day-to-day items, which are influenced by her daily life experiences. The people she meets, places she visits and activities she tries all play a part in her work, and she finds endless motivation for these projects from talking to other creatives who are passionate about what they do. Mathers enjoys the problem-solving aspect of creating her pieces. She starts a project by considering what details she would like to highlight, the best way to make it and how simple or complex she would like the finished piece to look. Her work is recognizable because of her graphic, geometric style, and she enjoys pushing the boundaries with paper to achieve more complicated projects, while allowing her skills to develop as she learns different paper techniques.

Think about which aspects of your everyday life most inspire you and write down a list of these things. Try drawing an object you associate with a memory or experience, and experiment with cutting and folding techniques to pay homage to it in paper form.

3D Collage

MIXED MEDIA #1

—

Collage is usually associated with flat 2D images composed from overlapping paper shapes. However, there is no reason why a collage cannot be a 3D image, and it doesn't have to be restricted to paper. Mixed-media artist Anne ten Donkelaar, based in the Netherlands, creates fantastical artworks she describes as flower constructions. Her 3D collages are made from pressed flowers, cut-out floral prints and photographs. Each element is carefully placed on pins set at different heights to achieve depth, making the image appear to float. Donkelaar says they are 'like a fantasy herbarium, filled with dried flowers or branches with irregular shapes, and some refer to planets'. Donkelaar's idea emerged when she pinned real flowers and floral images onto a mood board created as inspiration for another project.

Create your own mixed-media collage by collecting materials, images and sketches related to a theme that inspires you. Cut out some shapes and experiment with different ways of layering and attaching the elements.

RIGHT:
Flower construction #86

OPPOSITE TOP:
Flower construction #95

OPPOSITE BOTTOM:
Flower construction #89

Letterpress

TECHNIQUE #1

—

Although technically considered a printmaking technique, letterpress printing involves texturing paper with low-relief impressions of inked raised surfaces: a printing press repeatedly compresses the paper against a bed of moveable printing plates. This 15th-century technique was the primary means of printing information until the 20th century, when it was replaced by offset printing techniques. In recent years, letterpress printing has undergone a revival among artisans, and today it is typically used by designers to embellish stationery and packaging with low-relief text and images.

El Calotipo Design & Printing Studio is a Spanish company specializing in letterpress, screen printing and stamping for packaging, stationery and editorial design. The examples of their work here show how they have applied unique, textured brand images to stationery, using the letterpress technique.

See if there is a letterpress workshop near you to explore this technique yourself. You could also purchase affordable desktop embossing machines and customized printing plates, which would allow you to achieve similar effects at home.

OPPOSITE TOP LEFT:
Villagomá Catering

OPPOSITE TOP RIGHT:
Cousa Rica

OPPOSITE BOTTOM:
El fotógrafo de Wedland

Self Expression

INSPIRATION #2

—

Challenging yourself to create something new daily is an incredible commitment, but can ultimately be very rewarding and help foster greater creativity.

Cristian Marianciuc, a paper artist from Romania, challenged himself to create a new origami paper crane every day. He records each one as a daily visual diary, and he aims to make a total of 1,000. Marianciuc views the creative process as a form of mindfulness and self expression, and says that, 'Each crane represents the emotions, thoughts and experiences of the day in which it was created.' Most start as simple, traditional origami cranes, then he adorns each differently, using a variety of materials and techniques, including papercutting intricate designs into the paper wings, or incorporating fresh flowers and other natural materials.

Set yourself a similar challenge and commit to practising a papercraft technique daily. Choose something that can be produced in many different ways so that you have the freedom to exercise and express your creativity.

OPPOSITE:
Decorated Crane 2

Exploring Texture

TECHNIQUE #2

—

OPPOSITE TOP:
Gardening

OPPOSITE
BOTTOM LEFT:
Song of the Sea

OPPOSITE
BOTTOM RIGHT:
Work in Progress

Based in the UK, Fiona Clabon's colourful paper designs are created by hand through a unique process using textured paper collage. She enjoys creating bright, bold and cheerful illustrations, intended to add a little joy, fun and colour to the home. While printmaking at university, Clabon found she loved the colours and textures produced when she pressed a piece of paper down onto rolled-out printmaking ink. She creates her collage designs by cutting shapes from these textured papers and experimenting with composition by layering them up in different ways. She then scans them into the computer to make final adjustments using design software.

Take photographs of some textures that inspire you; they could be anything from rust on the side of a boat to peeling paint on an old door. Experiment with different combinations of materials and painting techniques to create textured marks on paper inspired by your images. Use these textured papers for your next project, perhaps a paper sculpture or collage.

Forests

INSPIRATION #3

—

There is something poetic about using paper to depict its own natural origin: trees. The intricacy that can be achieved with papercutting techniques really lends itself to exploring details and shapes of treetops silhouetted against the bright sky. Artist Gaby Studer, based in Schöfflisdorf, Switzerland, takes direct inspiration from the trees, forests and landscapes in her surroundings to create her papercuts. She works from sketches or photos, and each detail is meticulously cut out from black paper by hand, using scissors. The final results are incredibly striking.

To achieve a similar effect and pay homage to the beauty of trees, take your sketchbook or camera with you the next time you take a walk in a forest. Document interesting shapes or textures and really take notice of any contrast between tree branches and sky. Later, outline your sketch or photograph onto tracing paper, then scan into your computer and print so that you have a template to create your papercut from.

RIGHT:

Up

gaby studer 2017

Lighting

APPLICATION #1

—

Paper is a wonderful material for experimenting with light and shadow, and its translucent quality really lends itself to lighting design. Paper lanterns originated in China many centuries ago and have since held a particular prominence in Asian culture. Techniques like folding, layering or cutting into paper can dramatically enhance the shadows cast by the light emanating from the lanterns.

Hannah Nunn is a UK-based artist who uses lighting design as a way to explore her appreciation for tiny details observed in nature and her surroundings. Nunn starts with observational sketches that she simplifies into silhouettes before scanning them into her computer. She then either laser cuts or engraves the shapes into paper to achieve different lighting effects. Finally, the paper is laminated to strengthen it. For Nunn, light is the magic ingredient and instantly brings her intricate designs to life.

Try experimenting with papercutting your own simple paper lanterns. Traditional, handmade Japanese washi paper would be an ideal choice for this project. Find a template for a 3D lantern then sketch the areas you would like to cut out.

Vintage Papers

INSPIRATION #4

—

Many of us are well aware of the importance of limiting our waste and helping to protect our environment by recycling or reusing materials.

Jennifer Collier is a UK-based artist who sees the value in the discarded and seeks to give unwanted materials a new lease of life by transforming them into something fresh and unique. Collier is inspired by found vintage papers, which she stitches together with thread and recycles into exquisite sculptures. These often take the form of familiar objects suggested by the narratives of the old papers used such as this sculpture of a watering can made from paper printed with vintage botanical illustrations.

Next time you're about to discard an old newspaper, magazine or book, have a look through for something that might spark some creativity. It might be an important issue discussed in an article, your interpretation of some beautiful text, or an image that is meaningful to you in some way; use this paper to create a new work of art inspired by its story.

OPPOSITE:
Paper Watering Can

Decoration

APPLICATION #2
—

Paper flowers are a very popular theme in the papercraft world and there are infinite styles and ways of making them. UK-based designer Laura Reed has become known for her stylized paper flower designs, although she works on a wide variety of papercraft briefs for clients. Inspired by natural flowers, vintage botanical prints and contemporary design, Reed starts a new piece by experimenting with drawing, cutting and assembling some initial shapes. She then draws the flat shapes digitally on Illustrator so that the petals can be cut out by her plotter (vinyl cutting machine). Then the flowers are shaped and constructed by hand, and Reed will continue to alter scale and shapes until she reaches a result she is happy with.

Make your own paper flower decorations by experimenting with some ideas for petal and leaf shapes on scrap paper. Once you have a clearer idea, edit and redraw your final petal shapes onto coloured paper ready to make your final paper flower.

LEFT:
Garland

People

INSPIRATION #5

—

John Ed De Vera, a designer from the Philippines with a passion for papercraft, creates paper portraits that draw inspiration from significant people and their prolific lives. De Vera says, 'My papercut portraits started when the news of David Bowie's death broke, I was so moved I created a paper tribute portrait of him. Now, every time someone makes the headlines and if the news somehow affects me, I create a portrait of that person.' De Vera makes his paper portraits entirely by hand, working from preliminary sketches. He describes his unique technique as a combination of kirigami and paper tole, which involves cutting, folding, sculpting and building up layers to create a 3D image.

You can create portraits from paper in infinite ways so experiment with different techniques or styles to find what works for you. Create sketches of people who inspire you and think about the colours and shapes you associate with them and their lives. From this point, explore how their facial features can be translated into a portrait using layers of paper.

Abstract Collage

STYLE #1

—

Cutting and collaging simple abstract shapes without planning an end result can be a great way to explore creativity; it is also a good starting point for someone who is new to working with paper.

Julie Hamilton is a surface pattern designer based in Canada, who creates abstract collage compositions, influenced by the colours, shapes and textures of nature. She uses watercolour and acrylic washes to make her own painted papers and experiments with different paper weights to achieve a variety of textures, cutting geometric and botanical inspired shapes from these using scissors. Hamilton says, 'I like to call it drawing with scissors. It is best not to pre-draw as that helps achieve the whimsical and slightly wonky nature of the pieces.' Preferring to work intuitively, she arranges the cut pieces on a large white background, moving elements around until she is happy with the composition. Try creating your own abstract collages, experimenting with different-coloured cut paper shapes.

OPPOSITE:
House On The Hill

Flowers

INSPIRATION #6
—

Flowers are a popular theme for paper artists due to the organic and fragile properties of paper. California-based artist Yang Liu creates beautiful, lifelike crepe-paper flowers, which draw inspiration directly from her subject matter. She usually starts her projects by studying either a live flower or botanical reference photos. She then works out a palette of papers and plans where she will need wire to support the curvature of a petal or leaf. Liu finds that cutting petals as individually as possible tends to yield the most natural results and using crepe paper allows greater manipulation of the material into more organic shapes. She says, 'When gluing petals to a central stem, it is very important to continue looking at reference material so the petal mimics a real flower.' Liu experiments with alcohol markers and wax pastels to achieve different colours and realistic details.

Try sketching a flower from life then recreating it as a paper model. Use wire for your stem, then cut out crepe-paper petal and leaf shapes to attach individually with glue. A coat of acrylic matte or gloss medium can further enhance your leaves to look more natural.

OPPOSITE:
Romance – Lilies, Roses and Peonies

Mixing Papercraft with Illustration

MIXED MEDIA #2
—

Paper is an incredibly versatile medium because it can be easily combined with so many other materials to create different effects and styles. US-based illustrator Lauren Paige Conrad creates mixed-media collages inspired by personal narratives and the mundane. She starts with a sketch, then uses gouache to paint paper in different shades. Next, she decides on a colour palette, cuts shapes out of the relevant painted paper and builds up her composition, moving parts around until she finds the right balance. She then sticks down the pieces and adds final details using graphite and coloured pencils. Conrad says, 'I think it's good to be surprised by yourself, to keep inventing new ways of making work.'

Look closely at something usually overlooked from your everyday life and sketch it, focusing on the individual shapes and how these work together. Choose some materials and use them to create different textures and colours on your paper. Use scissors to cut the shapes and assemble them, gradually rebuilding the image from your sketch. Add details using your tools once you're happy with the layout of your piece.

Entomology

INSPIRATION #7

—

Like many other talented creatives, Lisa Lloyd, who is based in the UK, is drawn to nature and it is the main inspiration for her paper sculptures. She is particularly curious about entomology: the study of insects. Lloyd explores pattern, symmetry, texture and colours in her 3D models, which are created entirely from paper and range from colourful butterflies to iridescent beetles. She uses thicker paper to shape her internal structures, then meticulously cuts out as many as 3,000 individual decorative details by hand from thinner paper; these give her pieces a lifelike quality and texture. Lloyd says, 'I feel like a wildlife photographer when I'm shooting the final pieces; I want my creations to look like they're alive. Capturing that feeling of flight or movement is really exciting and a big part of my work.'

If you have a macro lens, photograph insects or sketch details straight onto paper. Alternatively, find royalty-free source material online or in a library to sketch from. Focus on an aspect or detail of the insect which you find especially interesting, and explore this using a paper technique of your choice.

ABOVE:
Chalcosoma beetle

OPPOSITE:
Bee

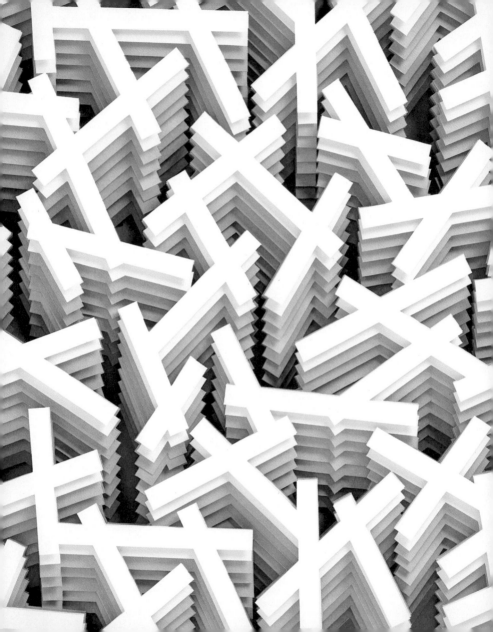

Exploring Pattern

TECHNIQUE #3
—

So many amazing patterns surround us, and artists have often drawn inspiration from those observed in nature or in the geometry of man-made structures. They can range from simple repeats of shapes and motifs to incredibly complex and ornate designs.

French designer Maud Vantours creates beautiful 3D paper sculptures that explore pattern and repetition of shape. Finding inspiration from her surroundings and the material itself, she cuts into layers of coloured paper to create her bold, patterned pieces, which often resemble hypnotic, dreamlike landscapes.

Look at the patterns around you and find a particularly interesting one. Sketch this shape multiple times, varying the scale and position, either by hand or by using digital tools such as Photoshop. Once you've completed your design, copy it onto a clean sheet of paper and cut out the shapes using a craft knife and cutting mat.

LEFT:
Lines

Traditional Papercutting

STYLE #2

—

Papercutting became popular in Germany and Switzerland in the 16th century, taking on the name 'Scherenschnitte', which translates as 'scissor cuts'. Traditional papercut silhouettes from this region often feature rotational symmetry within incredibly intricate designs and are cut from black paper.

Marc Schweizer is an artist from Switzerland, who has been practising papercutting since he was taught by his mother when he was eight years old. Over the years, his work has developed to feature a combination of traditional and non-traditional elements, influenced by his skills as an architect. The raw beauty of the Swiss Alps can often be seen in his pieces and he has adopted the traditional symmetrical style of Scherenschnitte by folding thin black paper in half before starting a design, so that his cut image creates a reflection of symmetry.

You can create your own traditional-style papercut by folding some thin paper in half, then drawing a design on one side of it. Use a craft knife to cut out your design. Once completed, you will be left with a beautiful symmetrical design.

OPPOSITE:
*Märchenlandschaft
(Fairytale Landscape)*

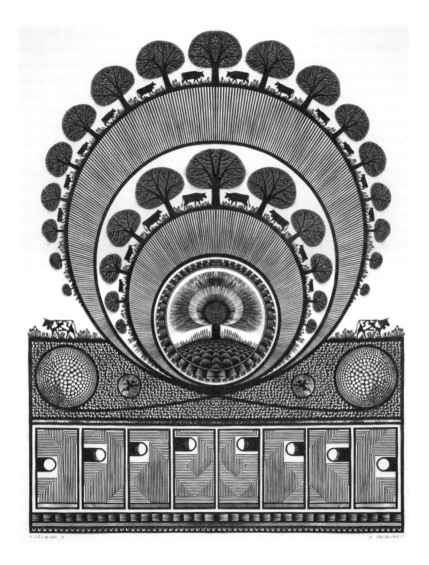

Paper Quilling

TECHNIQUE #4
—

Paper quilling – which involves twisting, curling and rolling narrow strips of paper, and manipulating them into decorative coiled shapes – has seen a real resurgence over the last few years, largely thanks to the handiwork of contemporary paper artists like the internationally renowned, UK-based Yulia Brodskaya. She constantly challenges herself to find new ways to practise quilling, with subjects ranging from typography to portraiture. She says, 'For these portraits, I use the technique that I created after a few years of experimenting and developing quilling techniques: I call it "painting with paper" because I'm imitating brushstrokes with tightly bent and packed strips of paper and card, but the difference is that these "brushstrokes" are three dimensional. Both portraits depict real people.'

Try creating your own images using quilling techniques. First practise the basics, then find a way of attaching curled or folded paper that works best for you and your style.

OPPOSITE:
Natasha Hastings

ABOVE:
Aleseia

Responding to a Brief

APPLICATION #3
—

3D paper art allows you to push the limits of paper, and with practice, very impressive results can be achieved. Paper modelling involves a lot of experimentation, so it encourages a certain degree of playfulness and imagination. It has become a popular contemporary design tool, one often used for advertising campaigns, editorials, animation and set design.

Berlin-based paper artist and art director OLLANSKI has spent just over a decade honing his paper-sculpting skills, and his long-standing passion for paper art has led him to some exciting projects. OLLANSKI has handcrafted paper objects in response to design briefs set by iconic brands such as Pepsi, PlayStation and Villeroy & Boch. He is inspired by a huge range of themes, but his unique playful style is instantly recognizable. He says, 'In an age of digital VFX and simulations, the ingenuity and versatility of my paper art gives my clients' advertising campaigns a real edge and an allure.' Try devising your own paper advertisement campaign images for your favourite brand.

OPPOSITE:
Raus ins Grüne
(Out into the Green)
for the *BARBARA*
magazine cover

Cultural Heritage

INSPIRATION #8
—

Indian papercut artist Parth Kothekar discovered papercutting during experiments with graffiti stencils, and he soon realized that this artform allowed him to feel a greater connection with his work. He says, 'I have seen that almost every culture in India, throughout time, has left its mark through heritage architecture. Such a level of intricacy carved into stones during a period that had no modern tools inspired a sense of reverence in me.' Papercutting is the ideal process for exploring and portraying intricate detail; Kothekar uses this technique to recreate complex, ornate patterns of the architectural monuments that inspire him, including the spectacular Havelis of Jaisalmer, Rajasthan, and various monuments of the Mughal era.

Reflect on your own cultural heritage and sketch observations of significant monuments or patterns, paying particular attention to any details such as carvings on the walls. To create a striking paper silhouette, score and cut out the details and design with a craft knife.

RIGHT:
Ornate Patterns of Indian Havelis

Geometric Sculpture

STYLE #3

—

Guardabosques studio, based in Buenos Aires, was formed by Carolina Silvero and Juan Elizalde. Working primarily in papercraft design and illustration, they create unique paper-based artwork for editorial, fashion, advertising and film in their signature geometric style. The studio enjoys translating what they have learned about a species onto paper, using their skills as designers to visually share their curiosity with other people.

To start a piece based on a real animal, Guardabosques collects a lot of related references in different angles and poses. The team starts modelling a design digitally, using 3D software or drawing in Illustrator. They then use paper-modelling software to draw templates that can be printed onto flat sheets of paper. The templates are cut from paper using a vinyl cutter, then folded, assembled and glued by hand.

If you're interested in creating some of your own 3D paper sculptures, try recreating an object that interests you, either using computer software to help you design a template or drawing and experimenting with 3D nets by hand.

OPPOSITE:
Amarula poster

Female Empowerment

INSPIRATION #9

—

In response to a growing pressure to 'fit in' and share only the best version of yourself on social media, there has recently been a more positive shift to honesty and openness. This is especially prevalent among female creatives, many of whom use their talents and imagery to convey how women really feel about unrealistic expectations placed on them about their appearance, relationships and life choices.

Poppy Chancellor is a UK-based illustrator who explores this theme through papercut illustrations. Her bold, distinctive style incorporates humour and sometimes bright colours to create relatable, memorable pieces. The contemporary subject of her papercut silhouettes breathes new life into traditional papercraft.

Reflect on a current issue that you feel passionate about and would like more people to be aware of. Experiment with bold lines and highlight important ideas with intricate details, really drawing the eye in.

BELOW:
Love Thyself

Miniature 3D Sculptures

TECHNIQUE #5
—

Rosa Yoo is a self-taught paper artist based in South Korea. She is especially interested in 3D paper illustration and creates delicately cut, folded and shaped miniature paper sculptures inspired by everyday life and objects. She enjoys including small details to give her paper objects character and bring them to life. Yoo says, 'I like to tell people a story about my experiences or memories through everyday objects delicately expressed in the material of paper.'

When Yoo has an idea for a new piece, she starts by sketching whatever has come to mind, then makes a more detailed template on the basis of the initial sketch. It can be difficult to accurately visualize how a 3D artwork might turn out, so Yoo recommends trialling the templates first. If the template doesn't work, Yoo finds out why and addresses any problems, editing the template and retesting until she successfully creates the shape she imagined. The template is then transferred to the paper so that each piece can be cut and assembled with glue.

Choose your own everyday objects to create a series of mini paper sculptures.

OPPOSITE:
Paper Miniature
Collection

Cities and Landmarks

INSPIRATION #10

—

Sam Pierpoint is an illustrator and paper artist based in the UK. She designs and handcrafts all of her eye-catching paper sculptures for a variety of purposes ranging from advertising campaigns and set design, to packaging and window displays. Pierpoint is inspired by places and enjoys observing the world around her, taking in its beautiful and often comical charm. Her most prolific pieces feature meticulously observed details inspired by memorable landmarks and buildings from cities she has visited.

Pierpoint starts by creating a sketch of the composition and generating a colour palette. She then translates elements of her sketch into 3D templates on software before cutting most components out on her cutting machine. She folds and joins each 3D paper object, until her initial idea is realized. This is then photographed, edited and sometimes animated to create the final piece.

Explore your nearest city or town, sketching interesting landmarks and inspiring aspects of the scenery. Use these sketches to design a scene that represents your chosen environment.

OPPOSITE:
Paper Bristol

Working with Layers

TECHNIQUE #6

—

Working with multiple paper layers allows artists to experiment with depth and texture. The technique requires careful consideration and requires more time to plan, but the exciting process can produce spectacular results.

Based in the UK, paper artist and graphic designer Samantha Quinn loves to work with layers to create texture and pattern within her vibrant paper artworks. Taking inspiration from her travels, experiences and memories, Quinn starts each new idea with a quick sketch to map out her composition and help her to think about the best way to infuse layers and depth. She designs some of her more complex pieces digitally, or hand-draws her ideas straight onto tracing paper to build up and consider her layers. Quinn transfers the design for each layer onto thin layout paper, which she lightly adheres to her chosen coloured paper stock. The designs are cut, assembled and then fixed into place using foam spacers or mount board to create depth and height between layers. Create your own layered project, carefully planning where each layer should go.

OPPOSITE:
Queen of Hearts

Combining Digital with Handmade

MIXED MEDIA #3
—

German illustrator Stephanie Wunderlich has a unique mixed-media approach to her beautiful editorial illustrations. Starting with a hand-drawn sketch, she traces the larger elements of her drawing, which she uses as a guide for cutting these shapes out. She sometimes glues the elements together, but usually scans them separately so that they can be rearranged later in Photoshop. Once she has decided on her composition and has positioned everything using her digital software, Wunderlich starts to work over her shapes, adding details to her collage with a combination of precise digital vector lines and textures. Digitizing her artwork in this way allows her to achieve a unique combination of handmade qualities and a crisp, technical appearance.

If you would like to combine digital and handmade processes, there are lots of design software tutorials available online. First design an image and cut out the basic shapes from paper then, using a scanner and Photoshop, digitize and assemble your cut shapes into an interesting composition.

OPPOSITE:
Allianz Roter Faden

Specialist Papers

STYLE #4

—

Sarah Dennis is a British paper artist who works in a beautiful illustrative style, creating stunning paper artworks that explore a wide range of themes. She creates each of her illustrations by hand, building up layers of coloured paper to create depth and shadow.

There are many paper types, colours and weights available, and varying these can alter the visual impact of an illustration. In this work, Dennis has experimented with metallic papers, using folding and shaping techniques to enhance the reflective-surface qualities of the paper. The metallic paper catches the light and draws the eye in, bringing certain elements to life, while adding a different dimension and texture to her pieces.

Experiment with different samples of specialist papers to explore how an unusual surface quality can alter the look of your style and designs.

OPPOSITE:
Kakapoo

Using Paper Stencils

MIXED MEDIA #4
—

Studio potter Tamara Bryan uses papercut stencils to apply decorative patterns onto her pottery. Inspired by the plants and wildlife native to her home, in the Pacific Northwest, USA, Bryan cuts silhouettes out from paper and Tyvek to create stencils. Using slip (wet clay combined with coloured stains and natural pigments), Bryan paints swatches of white onto the surface of her ceramics. Once this is dry, she places a wet stencil on top, smoothing it down with a rubber rib, then uses a sponge to wipe away all the excess slip around the stencil. When she pulls the stencil up, there is an image imprinted onto the clay in the shape of the stencil. In this way paper becomes an inherent part of her artistic process and the combination of different creative techniques adds a unique dimension to her work.

Think about how using paper could add something fresh and unique to your artwork and enjoy experimenting with a mixture of different materials, using the strength of their properties to work together.

OPPOSITE:
*Stoneware mugs
and pitchers*

Using Pattern Designs for Products

APPLICATION #4

—

OPPOSITE LEFT:
Dragon Fruit

OPPOSITE TOP RIGHT:
Eucalyptus Bloom

OPPOSITE
BOTTOM RIGHT:
Sunday

Incorporating handmade elements into digital processes allows you to make interesting patterns with unique textures. Once a design has been digitally finished and transformed into a technical repeat-pattern tile, it can be applied to multiple surfaces or products such as gift wrap or stationery.

UK-based contemporary designer Tom Abbiss Smith creates abstract pattern designs for a variety of products. He starts by hand, cutting and tearing paper shapes. Next, he creates textures, patterns and marks on paper using printmaking and painting techniques. He then scans these onto his computer. Finally, the chosen elements are combined and manipulated using digital software to create a composition or pattern.

Design your own motifs and cut them out from coloured and textured papers, scan some onto your computer and experiment with compositions and patterns using digital software. A printing company can reproduce your digitized designs onto your own cards, stationery or gift wrap.

Paper Embossing

TECHNIQUE #7

—

Embossing is the process of creating a raised relief image on the surface of paper and is a subtle, yet effective way to add texture and dimension to a design. Artist Caryn Ann Bendrick is especially drawn to the tactile nature of paper embossing and the compositions for her embossings are first hand-gouged into the surface of a linoleum block. Bendrick then soaks paper with a high cotton content in water. The block and wet paper are then run together through a tabletop relief press, pushing the pulp into the carved grooves of the linoleum block. To prevent the paper from warping, the embossings are stretched until dry and the paper is left with a raised image of the original composition.

It is possible to try paper embossing without a relief press. Lay cotton paper on top of a stencil, then lightly mist with water. You can then use an embossing tool (stylus) to push the damp paper into the grooves of the design.

ABOVE TOP:
*My Love is Blind:
Plate 9*

ABOVE BOTTOM:
*My Love is Blind:
Plate 6*

OPPOSITE:
*My Love is Blind:
Plate 9*

"My Love is Blind: Plate 9"   9/10   Carys Ann Bendrick 2013

Hand-printed Wallpaper

APPLICATION #5

—

Before the industrial advancements of the 19th century, ornate and decorative patterns were printed onto rolls of wallpaper by hand. Contemporary artisan studio Addicted to Patterns, founded by Justyna Medoń and Mani Swiatek, takes this traditional craftmanship approach, specializing in designing and creating bespoke collections of screen-printed, nature-inspired wallpapers. Medoń says, 'People, process and passion brought us where we are today, enjoying every moment of the creation; from drawing, colour matching and hand-painting every single wallpaper background to printing layer by layer, it is meditative and it is addictive.' Valuing eco-friendly design, Medoń works with eco paints and is careful to reduce waste during the screen-printing process.

Medoń runs printmaking courses from Spike Print Studio in Bristol, UK. She teaches the fundamentals of pattern design and the screen-printing process, demonstrating how to create repeat pattern designs. Next time you decorate, consider designing your own wallpaper.

OPPOSITE:
Sea Florals wallpaper

Satellite Imagery

INSPIRATION #11

—

Aerial photography and satellite imagery both provide a digital view of the Earth from above. State-of-the-art technology delivers incredibly majestic and detailed snapshots of our planet, and the rich textures and colours produced can be a huge source of inspiration. US-based artist Amy Genser creates expressive textured artworks, combining colourful paintings with layered, rolled and cut paper. Her pieces are organic and evocative of natural forms, and bring to mind satellite imagery and aerial landscape views of vast oceans, rock formations and coral reefs. Genser uses paper as pigment to explore her fascination with the movement and flow of water and the organic irregularity of the natural world.

Satellite imagery showing beautiful images of the Earth from above is accessible both online and in many artist reference books. Explore this theme and try out a variety of papercraft techniques using these resources as inspiration for the colours, composition or textures of your paper artwork.

RIGHT:

Intercoastal Blue

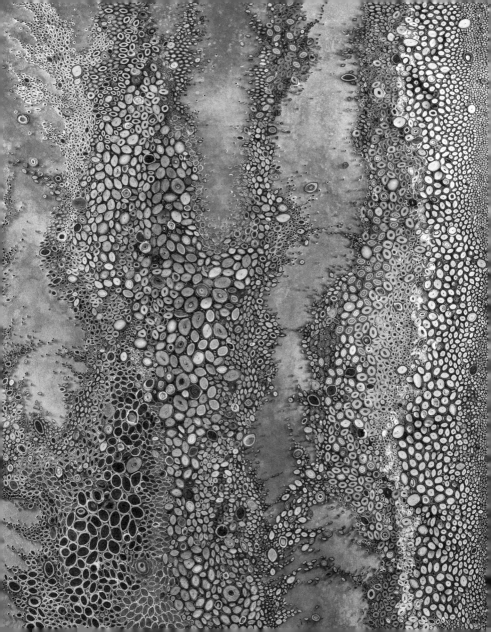

Bookmaking

TECHNIQUE #8

—

OPPOSITE TOP:
1–2–3 Stitched Booklets

OPPOSITE BOTTOM
LEFT:
Buttonhole-stitch Binding
(work in progress)

OPPOSITE BOTTOM
RIGHT:
*Long-stitch
Binding* (detail)

The craft of bookbinding has evolved considerably over time and many binding methods have arisen in different cultures, from the decorative stitches of Japanese binding to the long-stitch binding method that originated in medieval Germany. Bari Zaki is one of several contemporary artists finding inspiration from traditional bookbinding techniques and taking the time to learn the traditional skills needed for crafting uniquely beautiful handmade books. Zaki says, 'I love creating structures for people to protect, organize and display their cherished correspondence, travel ephemera and photos.'

Try this technique yourself, referring to bookbinding project books or online tutorials for more specific instructions. Before starting your own handmade book, consider its purpose and choose your paper type and weight accordingly. For example, if making a sketchbook, it is best to use thick cartridge paper. Experiment also with different paper types for your cover, or even make your own paper for it (see page 128–9).

Floral Patterns

STYLE #5

—

Tracey English is a UK-based illustrator and surface-pattern
designer who takes inspiration from nature to create whimsical
paper collages of colourful floral patterns. English paints all
her paper to achieve a wide variety of colour and textures
to use in her designs. She starts either with a rough sketch
or works straight from an idea, choosing her colours before
cutting the shape she needs from her selection of painted
papers, using scissors. She spends time arranging these into
patterns or compositions, then scans the designs into the
computer and finishes up in Photoshop. This enables her to
digitize and translate her work onto gift wrap, greetings cards
and home decor items.

Experiment with painting your own paper to create a colour
palette. Design some simple floral motifs and cut out repeats
from your paper. Arrange your shapes into patterns,
alternating colours and textures to create different results.

OPPOSITE:
Cornfield

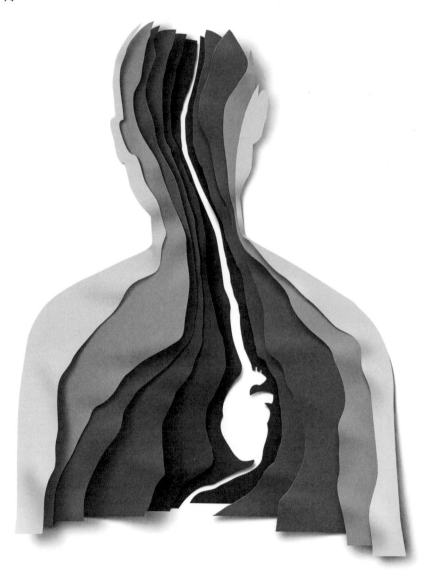

Editorial Illustration

APPLICATION #6

—

Talented illustrators like Eiko Ojala are often commissioned by publications to create eye-catching images in response to a story or feature. Based between Estonia and New Zealand, Ojala is especially known for his clever and witty editorial illustrations, which have a distinctive handcrafted appearance. He achieves this memorable visual style by initially drawing designs by hand. These are then transformed into papercut illustrations, which he either photographs or scans into his computer, enhancing original textures and shadows using Illustrator. Ojala tries to keep his work as minimal and precise as possible so that it works in harmony with the topic. He pays close attention to the fundamental forms of shapes and explores light and shadow to create a greater illusion of depth within a composition.

Develop your illustration skills and style by sketching designs in response to news stories that particularly spark ideas and creativity. Play with the theme using different papercrafting techniques to give your illustration a unique appearance.

OPPOSITE:
Heart Attack for the
New York Times

Paper Relief

TECHNIQUE #9

—

Brazilian paper artist Carlos Meira designs and creates sculptural paper relief illustrations, built up from layers of textured, raised paper. Inspired by traditional Japanese paper folding (origami), Meira uses various tools to manipulate and bend the edges of his cut paper shapes, adding some subtle 3D relief and dimension. He starts a piece by sketching his composition, then traces each separate element onto tracing paper. He transfers these tracings onto heavier paper using pencil, then cuts each shape by hand using a craft knife, cutting out the smaller internal details first. After Meira has added relief to the paper shapes, he builds his composition, gradually layering up the pieces like a jigsaw puzzle, fixing and lifting each individual layer with glue.

Do your own experiments with embossing tools and a bone folder to bend, curl and fold paper in different ways. Sketch a composition then build up an image using paper-sculpting techniques to manipulate layers of cut shapes. Use glue dots or 3D foam squares between your layers to add more relief to your piece.

OPPOSITE TOP:
Shipwrecked

OPPOSITE BOTTOM:
Flying

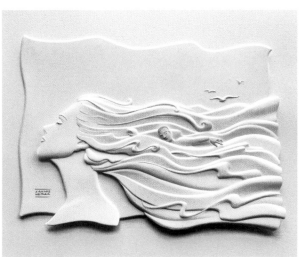

Dreams and Inner Worlds

INSPIRATION #12

—

Dreams can be an incredibly rich source of inspiration. Eugenia Zoloto is a Ukrainian paper artist who consistently explores this theme in her imaginative paper artwork. She creates giant, yet delicate, lace-like papercut pieces, very much influenced by dreams and her own thoughts and feelings. Zoloto additionally finds endless inspiration from nature and weaves complex arrangements of stylized flowers, insects and animals into her enchanting narratives, all of which she patiently cuts by hand using a craft knife. The large scale of her work encourages you to look closer and really appreciate all the details she incorporates into a piece.

Sketch ideas for a papercut silhouette influenced by your own imagination, perhaps drawing inspiration from your dreams. Think about the theme of your piece and the motifs you could include to reflect this. Ensure that your drawings all connect up, so that when it comes to cutting out your piece, you don't lose any elements of your design.

OPPOSITE:
Two Crows

ABOVE:
Delicacy

Repetition

TECHNIQUE #10

—

Many different outcomes can be achieved simply by repeating combinations of geometric shapes and folds. Using precise handcutting and folding techniques, artist Clare Pentlow creates highly detailed, mesmerizing pieces of art through methodical repetitive motions; building layer upon layer of paper. Pentlow, whose work has been exhibited across the UK, enjoys exploring the versatile qualities of paper, embracing both its strength and fragility within her pieces. Her process involves repeating a specific shape, cutting and folding it in the same way throughout. A pattern is created as she repeats the process in circles, layering and varying colours to achieve different effects.

Draw a simple shape several times, then experiment with cutting or folding it in varied ways. Design a piece that involves the repetition of this shape or certain colours and experiment with changing the scale of your shapes and the number of layers you use.

OPPOSITE TOP LEFT:
Mimas

OPPOSITE TOP RIGHT
AND BOTTOM:
Glacial

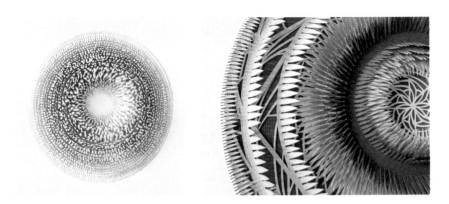

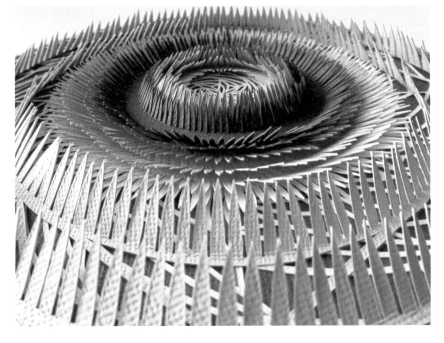

Character Art

STYLE #6

—

Creating artwork based on observations of the different characteristics, gestures and facial expressions of individuals can be both a challenging and interesting exercise. Based in Italy, Emanuele Tarchini is a paper artist who finds inspiration predominantly from everyday life experiences. He recycles and transforms paper into delicate sculptural figures and characters that have a story to tell. Tarchini's paper figures are often born of a personal idea or a fleeting inspiration and he starts his artwork from this point, firstly drawing his character in pencil, then cutting out each individual shape with scissors. He then patiently folds and manipulates each paper element before carefully assembling and gluing them together.

Take a sketchbook to a park or other public space and make observational sketches of the people around you (or recreate characters from well-known stories). Think about what makes them unique and draw on this in your character sketches. Finally, sculpt them from paper using different paper-modelling techniques.

OPPOSITE:
So Big So Small

ABOVE:
With the Wind

Photographing a 3D Paper Scene

TECHNIQUE #11

—

Fideli Sundqvist is a talented paper artist and image maker based in Sweden. Initially finding inspiration from traditional papercuts, Sundqvist began her career working with 2D paper silhouettes. She then went on to experiment with 3D paper techniques and now works predominantly with constructing 3D paper objects, which she arranges into colourful scenes to be photographed, like the image pictured here. She says, '*Penguin Beach* is one of several photos in a series of plant and animal images I made together with the photographer Magnus Cramer. These pictures are printed onto large glass plates that are the walls in a pedestrian and bicycle tunnel.'

Sketch a composition, then create some paper objects for your scene with 3D paper-modelling techniques. Construct your paper set then use a digital camera to capture this as an image, which can then be edited or enhanced as you wish, using computer software such as Photoshop.

OPPOSITE:
Penguin Beach

Storytelling

INSPIRATION #13

—

Fairy tales and folk stories have inspired artists of all disciplines for centuries, and can provide a rich source of ideas for paper art, too. Georgie Monica, who is based in the UK, creates uniquely illustrated paper cut-out scenes from such stories and says that the piece shown here is inspired by the Scottish and Irish folktales of selkies or 'seal wives': women who appear as seals in the ocean, but shed their seal skins to walk on land. 'Fishermen would take the skins and thus the selkies would become their wives.'

After painting the illustration onto different sheets of paper, Monica cut and constructed the entire piece by hand. For the furniture, nets of basic 3D shapes were created then folded into structurally sound objects. The characters are 2D paper cut-outs with some layered paper-relief details.

Find a folk tale that inspires you in some way and sketch what you imagine the characters look like. Draw your favourite scene then cut out different layers to create a collage or papercut from your design.

OPPOSITE:
The Seal Wife

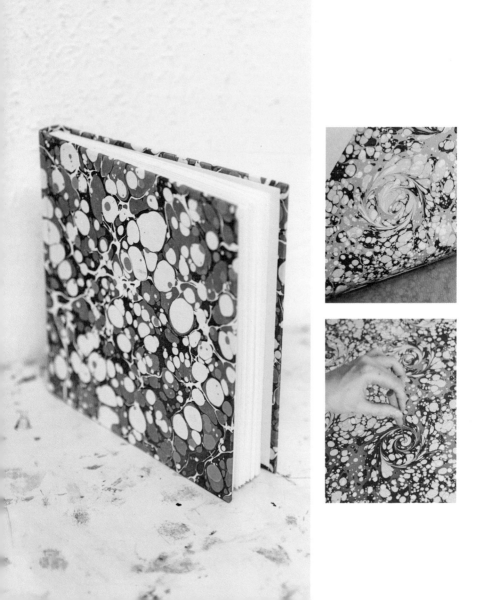

Paper Marbling

TECHNIQUE #12

—

OPPOSITE LEFT:
Turkish Stone sketchbook

OPPOSITE TOP RIGHT:
French Curl on paper

OPPOSITE BOTTOM RIGHT:
French Curl in motion

Paper marbling is the floating of combinations of paints or inks on an aqueous surface, usually made up of a base of water and suspension mixture known as a 'size'. The floating paints are swirled into patterns using marbling tools, so that when paper is placed onto the surface of the liquid, beautiful and unexpected effects can be achieved.

Balancing the variables correctly is an important aspect of marbling. UK-based Freya Scott, who produces exquisite marbled papers, says, 'Each type of paint behaves differently, e.g. watercolour will work differently to acrylic, and then within each type, the different colours will need mixing differently according to the properties of pigment and binder used. Because of this, many marblers choose to make their own paints, and I certainly make some so that they will behave properly with the others.'

You can find many tutorials and tips on paper marbling for beginners online. Experiment with different mixtures of paint types and size solutions, using a colour palette you love.

Paper Engineering

APPLICATION #7

—

Paper engineering is a discipline that explores design beyond the 2D realm, using cutting and folding techniques to transform flat sheets of paper into carefully constructed 3D objects.

Sarah Louise Matthews is a paper engineer based in the UK. She works with a variety of clients to design and make unique paper creations for photo shoots, visual merchandising and events. She predominantly draws her designs in Illustrator, working out the templates using a combination of maths, experience and experimentation. She then cuts out the individual pieces using her vinyl cutter, refining smaller details by hand. Matthews says, 'I hand assemble each piece – folding, gluing tabs together, shaping using a bone folder and whatever else is needed to create the piece. Often with 3D forms there will be an experimental stage in the middle, making maquettes to test and refine the design, learning from my mistakes and trying again.'

If you would like to experiment with paper engineering, there are plenty of 3D templates and tutorials available online.

OPPOSITE TOP:
Flamingo

OPPOSITE
BOTTOM LEFT:
Oranges

OPPOSITE
BOTTOM RIGHT:
*A Partridge in
a Pear Tree*

Contemporary Papercutting

TECHNIQUE #13

—

Papercutting is believed to have originated in China in the 4th century CE where it was predominantly used for religious decorations. The artform spread across different cultures, taking on many forms, purposes and styles over time. It is widely practised and remains a popular technique worldwide.

Wales-based papercut artist Georgia Low's distinctive contemporary papercut artworks are highly detailed. She sketches new ideas into a notebook before drawing out the final design onto 160gsm paper. She then meticulously cuts it out with a scalpel, carefully removing the cut pieces to gradually reveal the papercut image. The images here are high-quality digitized versions of Low's scanned originals, so that the designs can be reproduced as limited-edition prints.

Create a mood board with images that inspire you, then sketch some rough ideas for a design. Refine your drawing then start cutting out the shapes you wish to remove using a craft knife and cutting mat. You could frame your artwork or use it as a decoration for an event.

ABOVE:
Japanese Vase

OPPOSITE:
South China Tiger

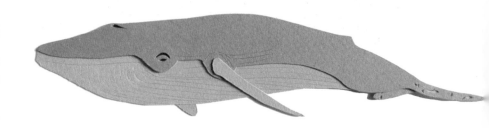

Wildlife

INSPIRATION #14

—

OPPOSITE TOP:
*Endangered Species
– African Wild Dog*

OPPOSITE BOTTOM:
*Endangered Species
– Blue Whale*

The animal kingdom is a visually rich source of inspiration for creatives and throughout time, different species have been studied and documented by a great many artists. Hannah Miles is a paper illustrator based in the UK who enjoys working by hand to create layered papercuts, as well as 3D papercrafted scenes inspired by wildlife and nature. Miles says, 'Driven to highlight some of the most endangered species, I choose a selection to research, then draw up shapes and grooves to recreate in paper. Each colour is a separate piece of paper, hand-cut and layered like a jigsaw to create the overall illustration.'

Find, photograph or sketch some images of animals to create a mood board. Pick one to create a paper design from then, after sketching your idea, choose a colour palette and papercraft technique to use for making your piece. Perhaps try building a 3D paper model of your animal, paying close attention to the form and textures; or if you prefer to work with flat paper, try collaging or papercutting your design.

Collagraph Printmaking

TECHNIQUE #14

—

Collagraph printmaking is a combination of collage and print: gluing textured materials onto a cardboard surface, then varnishing everything securely in place to create a collagraph plate. When this is dry, the plate is covered with rolled printing inks and placed face down onto paper. The paper and plate are then pressed together in a printing press to create an imprinted image of the collagraph plate. Each print differs slightly, depending on the amount of ink, paper type and pressure applied.

The prints here were created by Gordy Wright, a freelance illustrator and printmaker based in the UK. He is influenced by nature and plays with narrative in his work, using a variety of traditional techniques to explore texture.

You can experiment with collagraph prints at home without a printing press. Push the inked plate face down onto paper, pressing evenly with your hands. Peel this back to reveal your printed image.

OPPOSITE LEFT:
Sitting Hare
collagraph print

OPPOSITE TOP RIGHT:
Blackbird on Branch

OPPOSITE BOTTOM RIGHT:
Sitting Hare
collagraph plate

Paper and Thread

MIXED MEDIA #5

—

Paper is a very adaptable material and can be combined with many different mediums to explore ideas and achieve interesting effects. Netherlands-based Hagar Vardimon is a fine artist known for her distinctive thread-and-paper works, which have been exhibited in galleries across the globe. Vardimon takes time to source the right image, largely choosing to work with nostalgic, vintage photographs from the 50s, 60s and 70s. Once Vardimon feels that she has found a story within the image, she uses a single embroidery thread to stitch into the photograph, connecting objects with geometric forms and patterns. Vardimon puts a lot of thought into trying to understand the relationship between objects and figures depicted in the image. She says, 'The photographs I'm working with are connected to the main subject, common to all my works; memories.'

Why not try combining paper with sewing to add a different texture and dimension to your work? Use a sharp needle to poke holes into your paper, marking out your design, then stitch different threads into your piece.

OPPOSITE TOP:
At the End of the Road

OPPOSITE BOTTOM LEFT:
Spots

OPPOSITE BOTTOM RIGHT:
There is a Totem in My Front Yard

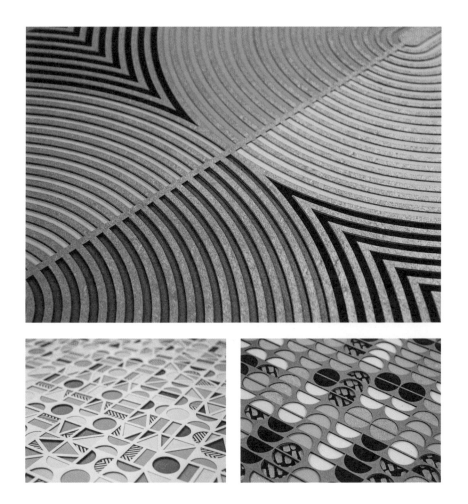

Architecture

INSPIRATION #15

—

OPPOSITE TOP:
Adjoin

OPPOSITE BOTTOM
LEFT:
Module

OPPOSITE BOTTOM
RIGHT:
Semi

It is no surprise that so many paper artists are influenced by architectural features and principles; the meticulously clean lines, stylistic qualities and carefully designed structures draw a parallel with the world of papercraft. Berkeley, USA-based designer Molly McGrath skilfully uses laser-cutting techniques to create unique paper artwork built up from layers of alternating coloured sheets of paper cut into bold geometric patterns. During her training as an architect, McGrath made architectural models using a laser cutter, which led her to realize the machine's unique potential to make jewellery and other intricately designed objects. McGrath began experimenting with the many creative possibilities of laser cutting, exploring different materials and creating a collection of contemporary papercuts, jewellery and homewares inspired by architecture.

Observe the architecture around you and sketch any details on building facades that capture your interest. Break down the shapes and arrange these motifs in different compositions and repeating patterns to create a 3D or 2D design.

Papercut Lightboxes

APPLICATION #8

—

Mumbai-based Hari & Deepti are a husband-and-wife artist duo who bring stories to life through their intricate papercut lightboxes. Their collaboration with paper and light began as an experiment in 2010 and they have since become internationally known for their signature backlit papercut dioramas. The process used for creating this magical artwork is inspired by the ancient art of shadow puppetry, a traditional form of storytelling in India and Bali. Each piece starts with a sketch, which is then broken down into various layers and hand-cut individually from separate sheets of paper. The layers are then carefully assembled into a light box and are divided by spacers of varying size to enhance depth and shadow. LED lights are added to bring out the intricate details and illuminate the artwork.

Try creating a papercut lightbox variation by building up a free-standing layered scene to be displayed with a light behind it.

OPPOSITE:
Nomadic Dwellers

Nature's Beauty

INSPIRATION #16
—

Paying close attention to the infinite details and colours within the natural world can provide endless inspiration for artists. Paper artist Hazel Glass, from Portland, Oregon, USA, celebrates the beauty of organic patterns and textures found in nature, translating her ideas into intricately layered, small-scale artworks. Glass says, 'The way our earth both wears down into underlying structures to reveal these patterns, and then builds up into new beauty from this deterioration, is truly mesmerizing to me.' Colour is also of great importance to Glass and the colour palettes she chooses are an integral part of her work. Glass hand-cuts up to 40 individual layers for each piece, stacking these up from her initial 2D drawing and attaching them with bookbinder's glue to create her precisely aligned relief sculptures.

Study the small details in the natural world, and record your observations of organic shapes and patterns in a sketchbook. Use these ideas to design paper artworks that evoke a sense of the natural wonder you were inspired by.

OPPOSITE TOP:
Nocturnal Vista

OPPOSITE BOTTOM:
Subterranean Sanctuary

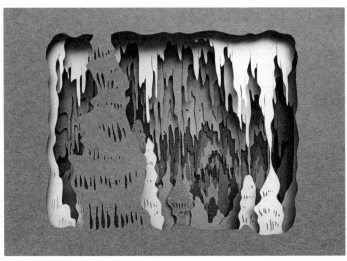

Small-scale Collage

STYLE #7

—

OPPOSITE TOP LEFT:
*Miniature Murder
on the Orient Express*
(based on Barnes
and Noble edition)

OPPOSITE
BOTTOM LEFT:
Jazz Band

OPPOSITE RIGHT:
*Edinburgh New
Town House*

The main premise of collage involves cutting, assembling and layering different flat shapes to build up an image. Collage can stimulate your creativity since it can be approached in so many different ways. UK-based illustrator Laura K Sayers uses small-scale papercut collages to skilfully explore a variety of themes. She prefers to use scissors freehand to cut out her paper shapes and challenges herself to make layered illustrations as small and detailed as possible. Sayers starts by planning a colour scheme, then draws out some rough sketches so that she has an idea of composition. She builds her tiny layers up using a pin to glue small pieces together, and adds the final details by applying gouache paint with a tiny brush.

Challenge yourself to make a freehand collage inspired by a theme that interests you and experiment with scale. How small can you cut your paper elements? Choose a selection of coloured paper and experiment with using either scissors or a craft knife to cut some practice shapes.

Personal Experiences and Identity

INSPIRATION #17

—

OPPOSITE TOP LEFT:
Litmus Garden II

OPPOSITE TOP RIGHT:
*'Xiang Lu III' –
Incense Censer III*

OPPOSITE BOTTOM:
Litmus Garden I

Paper artist Jacky Cheng was born in Kuala Lumpur, Malaysia and is currently based in Australia. She creates autobiographical paper artworks, which combine complex woven paper sculptures with printmaking processes and installation. Her desire to become an artist was influenced by the cultural ceremonies she remembers from her hometown. Cheng says, 'My Ah Ma (Grandma) was the first person that introduced me to paper. I would always be sitting by her side folding joss papers (spirit papers) for the afterlife in ritualistic ceremonies.' Her awareness of her grandmother's lost skill pushed her to realize the importance of cultural practices and authentic ancestral skills in preserving her identity. The skills gained in Cheng's architectural studies also influence the construction and style of her intricate pieces.

Think about how your cultural experiences inform your personal identity and draw shapes and forms that you feel best reflect this. Design a paper artwork incorporating these ideas, exploring cutting, folding and weaving techniques.

Craftsmanship vs Machine Precision

STYLE #8

—

Julia Ibbini is an artist based in the United Arab Emirates, who explores the juxtaposition of contemporary digital design, using computer algorithms, with traditional ornament and craftsmanship. She laser cuts her intricate designs to achieve machine precision, retaining a distinct human quality due to her cultural influences. She says, 'I use ornament and pattern as a way to document my experience with sources ranging from electronic music, Arabic geometry, embroidery and topographic contour markings.' Ibbini's pieces all begin with a single line and a circle, which are built into digital units that she transforms into larger drawings using software tools. The completed components of her drawings are then cut from numerous layers of paper using a customized laser machine. Finally, each part is glued by hand and combined with ink poured over Mylar to create Ibbini's trademark intensity of colour.

Try combining digital and analog processes in your own work to achieve a unique style.

OPPOSITE:
The Sublime Line

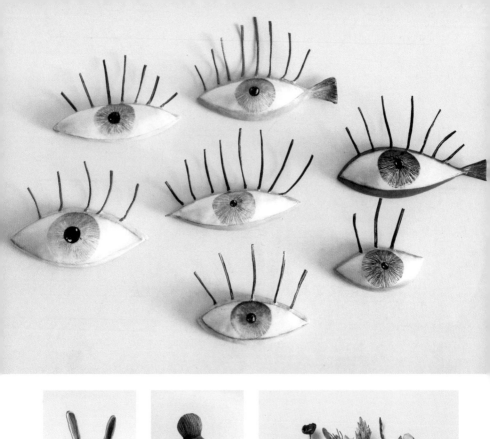

Papier Mâché

TECHNIQUE #15

—

OPPOSITE TOP:
Olho

OPPOSITE
BOTTOM LEFT:
Silencio

OPPOSITE
BOTTOM CENTRE:
Alma

OPPOSITE
BOTTOM RIGHT:
Corazon de Papel

Papier mâché is a papercraft technique that dates as far back as the Han Dynasty in China, not long after papermaking itself began. It was originally used to create ceremonial masks and warrior helmets. It has more decorative purposes today, often used to build large-scale carnival floats or theatrical props and costumes.

Argentinian artist Juliana Bollini uses the technique for sculptural purposes, modelling unique characters and dreamlike pieces adorned with whimsical painted decorations. Once Bollini has an idea for a piece, she constructs a wire base shape, and gradually builds up layers of paper strips and glue onto it. She alternates this technique with the other method of making papier mâché, which involves modelling elements of her pieces with a specially prepared dough made up of shredded paper and glue.

Use papier mâché to create your own sculpture. Sketch a design, create the basic shape in 3D using a wire structure or balloon and then apply layers of paper and glue. Once dry, decorate your sculpture with acrylic paints.

Greetings Cards

APPLICATION #9

—

OPPOSITE TOP:
Blue Fox

OPPOSITE BOTTOM
LEFT:
Favourite Things

OPPOSITE BOTTOM
RIGHT:
Honey Bee

Greetings cards are an increasingly popular design application that can also be considered as a form of papercraft. Karen Davies is a graphic designer and self-taught papercutter based in the UK, who creates handcrafted papercuts inspired by wildlife. She has developed a digitally printed collection of greetings cards featuring her most popular papercut designs. She varies her paper types and colours, carefully cutting out the positive spaces inside her design outlines, using a scalpel. Davies uses two processes to transfer her artwork onto cards: she either scans in her piece at a high resolution, or redraws the outlines of her designs using Illustrator, allowing her to digitally fill the design with a variety of colours. For both processes, Davies then sets up artwork PDF files on Illustrator ready to send to the printers.

You could create your own greetings cards using a process similar to Davies', or why not try experimenting with laser cutting your designs directly onto the card stock?

Block Printing onto Paper

TECHNIQUE #16
—

Originating in China, block printing is a technique used for printing text, images and repeat patterns onto textiles or paper. Traditionally, relief images were carved into wood, but today many artists use linoleum (lino). Based in Portland, Maine, USA, artist and printmaker Katharine Watson creates block-printed stationery and greetings cards adorned with bold, floral designs. She sketches her designs directly onto a lino block, which she then hand carves using lino-cutting tools. She then rolls oil-based printing ink onto her design block and transfers her image onto watercolour paper using an antique printing press to compress the paper against the inked surface of the relief image.

Block printing is an excellent way to explore repeat pattern on paper and you don't need access to a printing press. Lino blocks, printing ink and carving tools are available from most art stores and you can apply pressure to the back of your lino block during the printing process with the back of a metal spoon.

ABOVE TOP AND OPPOSITE:
Floral

ABOVE BOTTOM:
Branches

Katharine Watson

Intricate Details

INSPIRATION #18
—

Pippa Dyrlaga is a UK-based paper artist who creates incredibly detailed papercut artworks, using traditional techniques to explore her subject matter – usually something from the natural world. Dyrlaga skilfully cuts her work by hand from a single sheet of paper, using a sharp scalpel. After drawing out a rough layout, she works in sections, adding freehand detail as she works to emulate textures and patterns such as the scales of a snake or individual feathers. Dyrlaga enjoys the slow, meditative process of papercutting and due to the fragility of paper, it can take her up to 150 hours to complete a piece. Creating such awe-inspiring paper silhouettes requires a great deal of skill, practice and patience.

The process is just as important as the final artwork, and if you're new to papercutting, it's important that you take your time and savour the rhythm and meditative flow as you work.

OPPOSITE:
Thread

ABOVE:
Biophilia

Origami

TECHNIQUE #17
—

Origami is the art of paper folding and is most closely associated with Japanese culture; its name derives from the Japanese words 'ori' (folding) and 'kami' (paper). Traditional origami doesn't involve any cutting or gluing, and sculptural objects are constructed by simply folding a single sheet of square paper.

Barcelona-based studio, King Kong Design, specializes in creating modular paper installations for home interiors using origami techniques. Studio founder Kinga Kubowicz is influenced by geometry, symmetry and colour gradients, which she has explored in her latest design project 'Moduuli'. Each Moduuli wall panel is made up of individually cut and folded paper tiles.

Origami project books or instructional videos are a good starting point for those interested in trying out this traditional craft. Square origami papers are available in a variety of colours and are the ideal thickness for paper folding.

LEFT:
Moduuli White
Paper Cloud

Hand Lettering

STYLE #9

—

Hand lettering is a popular area of design, and some designers take it further by creating tactile 3D models or paper collages of letters. Matisse Hales based in Utah, USA, creates colourful cut-paper letters in a variety of styles. She starts each piece with a black-and-white sketch, which she refines into a template. Hales then decides on a colour scheme and cuts the paper either by hand or using a papercutting machine. Smaller details such as floral motifs, are sometimes cut from the body of her letters, or added onto the exterior in different colours. The pieces of her letters are assembled and secured into place with silicone glue, which also adds relief and dimension.

Create a mood board of hand lettering styles that inspire you, then draft your own letters onto squared paper. Sketch further details within your letter shapes and decide whether you would like to cut these away or collage onto your piece. Use your sketch as a template, taping it onto your chosen paper and cutting into both layers using scissors or a craft knife. Assemble the cut paper shapes to form your letter, using glue dots to secure layers.

ABOVE:
Blossoming B

FAR LEFT:
Lacy L

LEFT:
Delicate D

Mark-making

TECHNIQUE #18
—

There are infinite ways you can create marks and textures on paper due to its versatility as a material. Based in Atlanta, USA, artist Lucha Rodríguez, explores the effects of light on paper by cutting, carving and sculpting subtle marks onto the flat surface using a knife. The marks she cuts form bas-relief images and patterns, which very slightly protrude from the surface, casting interesting shadows. Rodríguez has a background in graphic design and printmaking, which influences the style of her artwork. She creates pieces across many disciplines, ranging from etchings, monoprints and colourful silkscreens, to immersive multi-layered installations of cut paper, each created with pink – the artist's signature colour.

Rather than drawing and cutting out a design, experiment with using different tools to create marks and textures on flat paper. To build up your design, combine a variety of marks, for example pierced or punched holes, cut curves and lines or embossed areas. Vary the scale of the marks, folding some areas to explore the effect of light and shadows.

OPPOSITE:
Knife Drawing
XV (detail)

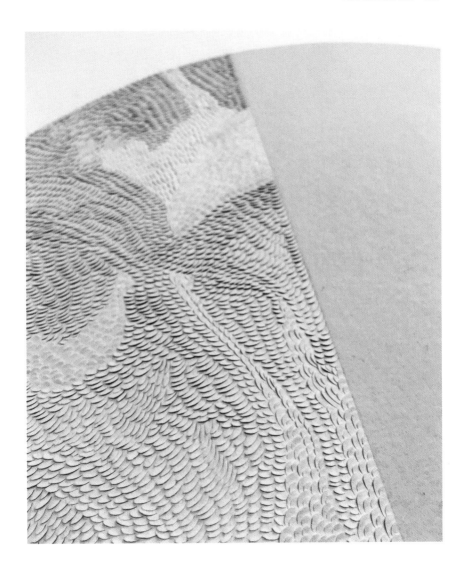

Iconic Buildings

INSPIRATION #19

—

OPPOSITE TOP:
Amsterdam

OPPOSITE BOTTOM
LEFT:
Russian

OPPOSITE BOTTOM
RIGHT:
Duomo

Iconic buildings are a great starting point for 3D paper projects, especially as there is so much reference material available online and in books. Prolific UK-based paper artist Hattie Newman, who builds large-scale paper sets, has recreated paper versions of some of the world's most recognizable and awe-inspiring buildings for her 'Canon city project'. Each paper building was placed into a square cityscape 3m × 3m (10ft × 10ft) in size, which was exhibited in Paris. Working on this project by hand allowed Newman to gain a greater sense of the different ways in which buildings are designed and constructed. After the exhibition, Newman worked with photographer Sun Lee to capture these images.

Make a list of some iconic buildings from around the world and gather up some reference material. Choose one that inspires you, and sketch the outline and individual shapes that make up the building. Design templates for your buildings by hand, experimenting with different outcomes, or you could use computer software to help you, and then 'build' your own iconic building.

Handmade Paper

TECHNIQUE #19
—

You can achieve some really interesting textures and experiment with different weights and thicknesses by making your own paper. May Babcock is an interdisciplinary artist based in Rhode Island, USA, who combines hand-papermaking with printmaking, sculpture and book-arts techniques. Babcock makes her paper by hand from foraged plants, recycled paper scraps and old cloth, turning these fibres into paper pulp using a specialist machine called a Hollander Paper Beater. She says, 'Working with the wet pulp, I embed seaweed, cast deep textures, showcase plant fibres, and sometimes even draw on the papers once they are dry.' Environmental information from specific sites, sketches of them and their history inform Babcock's pieces, which she installs and exhibits as public artworks across the United States.

If you would like to try making paper by hand, you can find techniques, videos and inspiration online, including Babcock's own www.paperslurry.com. Hold onto paper scraps from other projects to recycle into beautiful handmade papers you can reuse to create new artworks.

OPPOSITE:
Artist Residency at
Guadalupe Mountains
National Park

Textiles

INSPIRATION #20

—

British artist Naomi Kendall developed a love for paper after following a creative career as a community artist in London, and draws her inspiration from textiles. She describes her unique, colourful paper artworks as 'woven' and it's clear to see why they are labelled as such. Kendall meticulously cuts each section of paper by hand, interweaving these one by one onto the backing paper. Although she chooses a colour palette at the start, the pieces are assembled organically and Kendall judges the colour balance as she progresses through an artwork. Despite the complexity of some of her pieces, the tools used are simple: a pencil, ruler, craft knife, scissors and glue.

Take a trip to your local museum and study the textile collections, observing woven details and the way yarn and thread overlap. Alternatively, seek inspiration from your own wardrobe, perhaps taking photographs of particularly interesting colour combinations or fabric textures. Use these to inform your work and experiment with different ways of recreating these patterns using paper.

LEFT:
Trelew

Jewellery

APPLICATION #10

—

Although not usually associated with wearable accessories, paper is actually a great material to use for creating unique jewellery due to its lightness and tactile qualities. The late Dutch artist Nel Linssen used textiles and paper as her medium and became well known for her sculptural paper jewellery. Inspired by rhythms and structures in the botanical world and early sculptural experiments, Linssen started creating folded paper necklaces and bracelets, which she continued to develop over the course of 30 years. Linssen used the best-quality paper for her pieces, allowing her to experiment with more complex folding and construction techniques. Her work can be found in jewellery collections in museums and galleries around the world.

Try designing some wearable paper jewellery of your own, selecting your paper carefully to ensure greater strength and flexibility. Experiment with different folding and construction techniques to create 3D shapes that can be incorporated into your design.

ABOVE:
Necklace

RIGHT:
Bracelets

Paper Clay Forms

MIXED MEDIA #6

—

Some ceramic artists choose to sculpt more delicate pieces from a mixture of paper and clay because they are attracted to the extra strength and durability the addition of paper provides. Paper clay is also known for reducing warping and shrinkage during firings and pieces are often more lightweight, which is ideal for more decorative artworks. It is made by mixing paper fibres with a liquidized form of clay called slip. When the paper clay mixture reaches a suitable level of plasticity, it can be used for throwing pots or sculpting.

Italian artist Paola Paronetto's distinctive ceramic vessels and lamps are made from paper clay. The beautiful pieces in her Cartocci collection are sculpted by hand and are inspired by natural forms and everyday objects.

It can be expensive to invest in the space and equipment required to create your own batch of paper clay, however, ceramic classes offer the facilities and expertise for you to explore this technique. Ready-made bags of paper clay are also available, which would enable you to experiment with this interesting combination of materials.

OPPOSITE:
Sufi lamps

Visual Communication

APPLICATION #11
—

Graphic design is used to communicate ideas and concepts visually in a memorable way, aiming to inspire and inform a wide audience. Owen Gildersleeve is an award-winning UK-based designer who has honed his unique style in recent years, bringing his graphic designs to life through carefully handcut paper layers and a playful use of light and shadow. He has worked with an array of international clients, completing commercial and personal paper-based projects that range from intricate cover illustrations, animations and large-scale sets to installations and window displays.

The multi-layered topographic artwork 'Grand Canyons' pictured was commissioned by *Time Out Los Angeles* and draws inspiration from the title. Multiple layers of white paper were raised at varying heights, then shot with soft lighting to enhance the shadows and define forms. Using a bold typeface, he then cut through the canyon layers to reveal layers of vibrant colour underneath.

Use topography to inspire one of your projects and experiment with text and colour.

OPPOSITE:
Grand Canyons
artwork for *Time
Out Los Angeles*

Modelling with Paper

TECHNIQUE #20

—

Barcelona-based artist Raya Sader Bujana works with paper for a living and creates artwork for a wide range of purposes, including stop-motion videos, sculptures and exhibitions. Many of her projects are influenced by a love of nature and the incredibly detailed pieces she creates utilize the skills she honed while studying architecture. Bujana says, 'I've always liked treating paper as a mouldable material, I think my technique is close to sculpting. Shaping, layering and moulding the paper to create volume and detail is important to me.' The paper models pictured are a series inspired by houseplants. She enhances some of the colours and smaller details using watercolour paints and spends a long time perfecting each remarkably lifelike miniature paper plant.

Try modelling your own paper object, making careful observational sketches first then choosing which coloured papers you would like to use. Take time to experiment with different sculpting and paper-modelling techniques to achieve something you feel best represents the object you have based your model on.

OPPOSITE TOP LEFT:
*Tiny Big House
Plants Series, Black
Cardinal Philodendron*

OPPOSITE TOP RIGHT:
*Tiny Big House
Plants Series, Ficus
Elastica Ruby*

OPPOSITE BOTTOM:
*Tiny Big
Houseplants Series*

Dioramas

APPLICATION #12

—

OPPOSITE TOP LEFT:
*Campfire and
Yellow Tent*

OPPOSITE
BOTTOM LEFT:
Sakura Picnic

OPPOSITE RIGHT:
Whale Island

A diorama can be either a full-size or small-scale 3D model, depicting a particular landscape, historical event or scene from nature. You can sometimes find dioramas in museums, displayed inside glass cases. Taiwanese designer Li-Yu Lin, based in Denmark, uses paper to construct charming colourful diorama landscapes. Lin says, 'Every paper mini world is like a parallel universe with its own story and life.' Lin uses 3D software to design and build the geometric foundations of his paper landscapes and gradually adds more illustrative details as the piece progresses. He encapsulates his miniature paper worlds inside glass bell jars, which enhances their magical quality, while allowing them to be held in your hand and admired.

Visualize a landscape or theme that inspires you in some way and sketch a design for your own paper diorama. Plan how you would like to display your paper world and calculate the dimensions of your piece. Design and test some maquettes for a base or use 3D design software to create a template.

From Paper to Textiles

MIXED MEDIA #7
—

Sarah Fennell is a UK-based textile designer who enjoys working and collaborating with well-known brands such as John Lewis to bring fresh prints to the market. She has a passion for colour and pattern, and begins her vibrant fabric designs with a paper collage. Fennell says, 'Collaging with paper is how I draw; it instantly provides colour and texture to my ideas, and is the vehicle for my ideas developing organically over a sketchbook page.' Fennell uses simple tools for her collaging process and loves to include the abstract offcuts from previous collages, which may otherwise be discarded. She sometimes finds the negative space left behind from a cut shape more interesting and often incorporates these unusual shapes into her designs. She creates her final designs from built-up layers of her scanned collages, drawing artistic inspiration for her engaging compositions from her daily life and her travels, and from Matisse to Marimekko.

Try playing with new ideas and compositions using paper collage and abstract offcuts. Incorporate different mediums and a wide range of textures to produce interesting designs.

OPPOSITE:
Daphne fabric

Paper Costumes

APPLICATION #13

—

Canadian paper artist Pauline Loctin uses a variety of folding, origami and cutting techniques to create large-scale 3D paper structures that playfully explore her keen interest in light and shadow. The images pictured showcase some of Loctin's stunning paper costumes created for her recent *Pli.é Project*: an impressive photo series shot in different city locations across the globe. The series combines dance and paper art, exploring the similarities between the ways bodies and paper can fold and unfold, expressing movement in different ways; the complex folds of her paper costumes effectively mirror the flexibility of each dancer. The types of paper were chosen specifically for every dancer, so that the paper dresses could be tailored not only to reflect their culture, location and style of dancing but also to fit their individual personalities.

Experiment with pushing the limits of paper's properties; trying different paper-folding techniques to achieve flexibility and movement. Next, try constructing large-scale pieces and explore creating 3D paper art that could be worn.

OPPOSITE LEFT:
Pli.é Project – Annalisa.
Dancer: Annalisa Cianci of Teatro dell'Opera di Roma

OPPOSITE TOP RIGHT:
Pli.é Project – Brooklyn.
Dancers: Yinet Fernandez Salisbury, Amanda Smith and Daphne M Lee of Dance Theatre of Harlem, and Dandara Amorim Veiga of Ballet Hispanico

OPPOSITE BOTTOM RIGHT:
Pli.é Project – Mai.
Dancer: Mai Kono of Les Grands Ballets

Freehand Papercuts

STYLE #10
—

OPPOSITE TOP:
Our Beloved King – Love

OPPOSITE BOTTOM:
*Our Beloved
King – Music*

It is not always necessary to begin a new project with a sketch and there are many paper artists who prefer the freedom of expressing their ideas freehand. Thailand-based artist Simona Meesaiyati created the papercut images pictured here to honour the late King Rama IX of Thailand; they are part of a series of nine papercuts depicting the things that King Rama IX loved. Meesaiyati chose to cut out the positive spaces from her artworks freehand, to reveal designs made up of the leftover negative space (the paper silouhette left behind).

Choose a subject that inspires you and write down key words related to it. Try cutting out freehand shapes from a flat sheet of paper that work together to depict the idea that is in your head, gradually building up an image from the remaining negative space. Mount your piece onto a contrasting colour to enhance the papercut you have made.

Large-scale Sculpture

APPLICATION #14

—

Dutch artist Peter Gentenaar has spent many years developing papermaking techniques that push the boundaries of the material. His understanding of paper and its properties has allowed him to create impressive 3D sculptural pieces that have become bigger and bolder throughout his career. Gentenaar's large, organic forms are built up from thin sheets of handmade paper, reinforced with very thin ribs of bamboo. After preparing the paper pulp by beating it over a long period of time, he stretches his handmade paper over a bamboo framework before it dries. He says, 'The paper shrinks considerably, up to 40 percent, and the force of this puts the non-shrinking bamboo framework under stress, just as a leaf when it dries in the autumn.' The mechanical aspects of this process fascinate him and he has custom-built vacuum tables, presses and paper dryers to enable further experimentation with paper.

Try working on a large scale, experimenting with other more resilient materials like bamboo to build supportive internal structures. Try different paper types and weights to find out which offers the most strength and flexibility for your design.

OPPOSITE:
Icelandic Poppy

Printmaking with Stencils

TECHNIQUE #21

—

Some creatives use stencils as part of their process and paper is the ideal material for creating these. Sophie Rae is a UK-based illustrator who creates vibrant and distinctive prints, building up her images using handcut paper stencils and layers of ink. Inspired by the unique shapes, colours and textures found in nature, Rae first sketches shapes onto paper, then cuts stencils from them using a craft knife. Next, she mixes a variety of colours and tones using printing inks with which to coat her roller ready for printing. After placing a paper stencil onto some paper or card, she applies the inked roller into the stencil space, building up rich layers of colour. Rae says, 'I repeat this with any other stencils, overlapping them. I love the immediacy of results with this process and you can always cover up bits you aren't so keen on, using the same stencil multiple times.'

Try making your own paper stencils by cutting out some simple geometric shapes. Like Rae, you can then mix different-coloured printing inks, use a roller to apply them over the stencils and create layers of colourful printed shapes on the paper underneath.

RIGHT:

Flamingo

Folk Art

INSPIRATION #21

—

Papercraft has long been associated with folk art in cultures around the world such as the colourful Polish *wycinanki* papercuts or the decorative tissue paper *papel picado* banners used in celebrations across Mexico. Stacey Elaine works in Norwalk, USA, using tissue paper to create intricate and vibrant papercut scenes depicting animals and plants. Clearly influenced by her love for the natural world, Elaine also draws inspiration from Mexican Folk art, Indian wood block designs, fashion and textiles. Enjoying the creative freedom of working intuitively, Elaine cuts all of her designs freehand from sheets of different-coloured tissue papers. She says, 'Because I don't draw my designs before cutting them, sometimes it can take a few tries to create the perfect shape or form that I'm looking for.'

Research traditional folk art designs and sketch some favourite motifs and shapes. Experiment with different variations to suit your own style, then design your own composition. Vary paper types and weights to achieve different effects and textures within your piece, using scissors to cut out the shapes you designed.

OPPOSITE:
Giraffes

Surrealism

STYLE #11

—

Surrealism was an artistic movement pioneered in the early 20th century, which aimed to explore dreams and the inner workings of the unconscious mind. Surrealist artists challenge the rational aspects of life and celebrate the strange beauty of the uncanny and unexpected.

Colombian artist Teresa Currea creates imaginative mixed-media artworks inspired by Surrealism. Currea says, 'Each piece is a unique universe, inspired in abundance by nature, presented in imaginary ways close to Surrealist ideas.' Currea draws all her characters and elements first, then cuts each piece out by hand, arranging her layers into unexpected compositions. For the artwork pictured, she disassembled the light bulb's interior and replaced this with some of her papercut drawings.

Let your imagination guide you as you try to create artwork inspired by Surrealism. Sketch some dreamlike characters and scenes for a collage then arrange the elements into compositions that challenge the expected.

OPPOSITE:
Hidden Red Flower

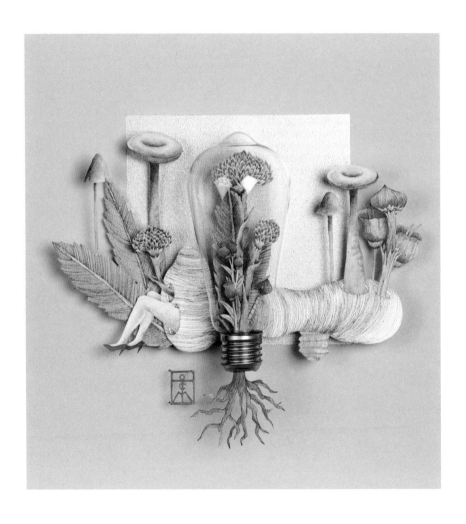

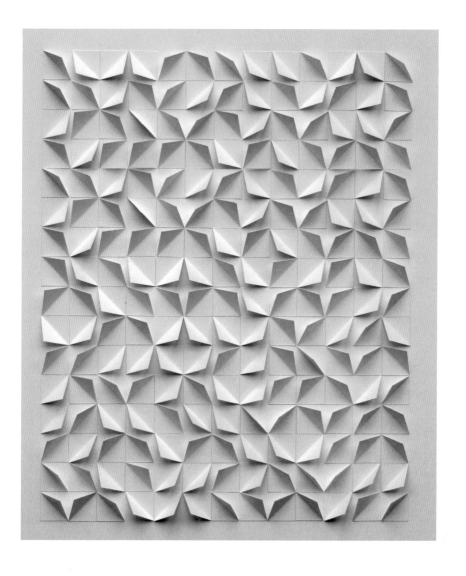

Light and Shadow

INSPIRATION #22

—

Tim van Eenennaam is a Dutch artist who methodically designs all of his paper artworks with light at the forefront of his mind. He finds inspiration from many places, particularly architectural elements and patterns created by sunlight falling onto a blank wall. Using a craft knife to partially and precisely cut repeat patterns of layered squares or triangles, van Eenennaam then systematically creates a variety of folds at different angles in order to catch the light and play with shadows. He starts a piece by drawing a repeating pattern on the back of the paper, and the corners of a shape or directions he decides to fold are often pre-determined by using a random number series to generate a sequence. He then uses bank cards to create crisp folds in the paper and experiments with different layers, patterns and scales to create a varied body of work.

Experiment with different papercraft techniques to create interesting shadows in your artwork. Fold and layer aspects of your design to build depth and enhance shadows. White, translucent or light-coloured papers are the most effective choices for this kind of work.

OPPOSITE:
Random Squares 7

Stop-motion Animation

APPLICATION #15

—

Since paper is such a flexible and versatile material, it lends itself well to animation projects. Vera van Wolferen is an artist and animator from the Netherlands who creates intricate and imaginative fantasy worlds out of paper, bringing their stories to life using stop-motion animation. Pictured here are some stills from her *Thoughthopper 3000* project, an interactive stop-motion animated website made entirely from white watercolour paper. Van Wolferen spends a long time designing papercraft sets in 3D software first. Once her computer model is finished, she uses software to transform the design into a blueprint for each object. Following minor adjustments, she adds final details in Illustrator before sending the blueprint to a cutting machine. Van Wolferen says, 'I animate by taking 25 pictures for every second of film. I animate mostly by myself, but I also work together with a stop-motion animator.'

Design your own 3D paper set, experiment with lighting and combine a sequence of photographic stills to create a simple stop-motion animation.

OPPOSITE:
Thoughthopper Kitchen

Geometric Shapes

INSPIRATION #23
—

Many contemporary artists are attracted to the simplicity and symmetry of geometric shapes. USA-based Israeli artist Yossi Ben Abu uses paper to explore these themes within his work. He has subsequently developed a modern and minimalist design style, creating precisely assembled geometric artworks inspired by architecture. Abu says, 'From a young age, I liked to draw geometric patterns based on architecture or interior design schemes. I would draw ideas from shop windows in Tel Aviv, old tiles and Moroccan motifs.' Abu usually starts by drawing a few sketches on paper, developing a design by creating a 3D version on his computer and varying both proportions and colour combinations. He then breaks up a final design into pieces that can be unfolded and cut from paper. Each piece is carefully folded back by hand then assembled into his final artwork on a white board.

Look for geometric shapes around you and sketch some patterns and motifs inspired by your observations. Use paper folding, layering and cutting techniques to create designs that celebrate the beauty of geometry.

OPPOSITE:
UnEven A

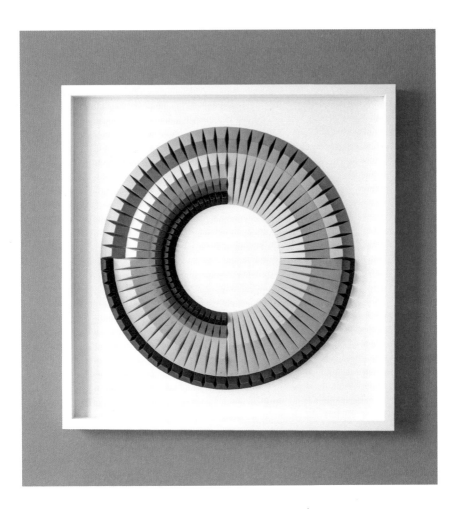

Cinema

INSPIRATION #24

The powerful storytelling and visual ingenuity of films can be a huge inspiration for creatives. UK-based collage artist Ben Giles creates imaginative artworks in response to ideas sparked by the unique aesthetics and themes of particular films. Drawn to highly stylized and choreographed sets, practical effect creatures and the charm of stop motion animation, Giles says, 'The stories themselves are interesting enough, but the hint of a larger canvas and the other stories within is always something I've been intrigued by.' Giles has built a varied collection of cut-out images, salvaged from vintage books and magazines, and he uses collage as a technique to explore concepts and ideas, building up striking, layered images.

Think about the films that are especially memorable to you and reflect on which aspects you are most drawn to. Is it the narrative which you find most interesting? Or perhaps the style of filming and cinematography fascinates you more. Try creating a poster for a film, using paper-crafting techniques to both capture and explore its theme and aesthetics.

OPPOSITE:
*Ray Harryhausen's
Dinosaurs*

Artist's Perspective

INSPIRATION #25

—

Although many artists like to work with paper in a precise manner, it can still be used as a great medium for expressing your emotions and imagination. Olga Skorokhod is a paper artist who creates beautiful layered and colourful 3D compositions inspired by nature's beauty and how she perceives it. Her pieces are not based on particular scenes; she says, 'I tried to give an impressive glimpse of what the beautiful world look likes through my eyes and imagination.' The main tool for creating her artwork is a scalpel and she applies foam pads between each layer to enhance the illusion of depth.

Visualize a particular aspect of nature that brings you joy and quickly sketch your interpretation of this. Choose a selection of coloured papers that reflect the mood associated with the scene and experiment with different papercraft techniques to achieve interesting textures and compositions. Try not to focus too much on how you want your piece to look at the end and work instinctively, so that the final piece becomes your own personal interpretation of nature.

OPPOSITE TOP:
Northwest Landscape

OPPOSITE BOTTOM:
Northwest Sunset

Sketching with Paper

TECHNIQUE #22
—

Traditional quilling or paper filigree work is a popular papercraft technique, involving twisting, curling and rolling narrow strips of paper to create an image made up of decorative coiled shapes. Inspired by this process, Judith, from American creative team JUDiTH+ROLFE, creates striking pieces from strips of paper but applies her own unique approach, turning each strip on its side so that its edge becomes a line in the image rather than building up an image from coiled shapes. She describes her way of working as sketching with paper and makes intricate artworks influenced by nature and flora. Judith prefers to make unmounted pieces, which requires her to glue the paper strips together rather than onto a background. This means that the final artwork can be framed between two sheets of glass to maintain an illusion of floating.

Experiment with treating paper as a sketching tool, manipulating coloured strips in creative ways to give your piece expression and movement. Try varying paper weights and thicknesses in your design, or rip the edges of your paper rather than cutting them to explore different line qualities and texture.

OPPOSITE:
Bloom

TOM ABBISS SMITH
P62–63
www.tomabbisssmithart.com

YOSSI BEN ABU
P160–161
www.yossibenabu.com

MAY BABCOCK
P128–129
www.maybabcock.com

CARYN ANN BENDRICK
P64–65
www.carynannbendrick.com

JULIANA BOLLINI
P112–113
www.instagram.com/julianabollini

YULIA BRODSKAYA
P40–41
www.artyulia.co.uk

TAMARA BRYAN
P60–61
www.tamarabryanpottery.
com

POPPY CHANCELLOR,
POPPY'S PAPERCUTS
P48–49
www.poppyspapercuts.com

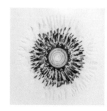

JACKY CHENG
P108–109
www.jackycheng.com.au

FIONA CLABON
P16–17
www.fionaclabon.co.uk

JENNIFER COLLIER
P22–23
www.jennifercollier.co.uk

LAUREN PAIGE CONRAD
P32–33
www.laurenpaigeconrad.com

TERESA CURREA
P154–155
www.teresacurrea.com

KAREN DAVIES, MUSTARD CUTS
P114–115
www.instagram.com/mustardcuts

JOHN ED DE VERA
P26–27
www.johned.co

SARAH DENNIS
P58–59
www.sarah-dennis.co.uk

ANNE TEN DONKELAAR
P10–11
www.anneten.nl

PIPPA DYRLAGA
P118–119
www.pippadyrlaga.com

EL CALOTIPO DESIGN &
PRINTING STUDIO
P12–13
www.elcalotipo.com/en

STACEY ELAINE
P152–153
www.staceyelaine.com

TRACEY ENGLISH
P72–73
www.tracey-english.co.uk

SARAH FENNELL
P142–143
www.sarahfennell.co.uk

AMY GENSER
P68–69
www.amygenser.com

PETER GENTENAAR
P148–149
www.gentenaar-torley.nl

OWEN GILDERSLEEVE
P136–137
www.owengildersleeve.com

BEN GILES
P162–163
https://benlewisgiles.format.
com

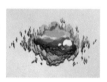

HAZEL GLASS
P104–105
www.artbyhazelglass.com

GUARDABOSQUES, JUAN NICOLÁS ELIZALDE
P46–47
www.guardabosqu.es

MATISSE HALES
P122–123
www.matissehales.com

JULIE HAMILTON
P28–29
www.juliehamiltoncreative.
com

HARI & DEEPTI
P102–103
www.harianddeepti.com

JULIA IBBINI, IBBINI STUDIO
P110–111
www.ibbini.com

JUDITH+ROLFE
P166–167
www.judithandrolfe.com

NAOMI J. KENDALL
P130–131
www.naomijkendall.com

PARTH KOTHEKAR
P44–45
www.instagram.com/
parthkothekar

KINGA KUBOWICZ,
KING KONG DESIGN
P120–121
www.kingkongdesign.com

LI-YU LIN, PAPIR LAB
P140–141
papir-lab.myshopify.com

PIETERNEL LINSSEN
(NEL LINSSEN)
P132–133
www.nellinssen.nl

YANG LIU
P30–31
www.shanghai1984.com

LISA LLOYD
P34–35
www.lisalloyd.net

PAULINE LOCTIN
P144–145
www.misscloudy.com

GEORGIA LOW
P92–93
www.georgialow.co.uk

CRISTIAN MARIANCIUC
P14–15
www.instagram.com/icarus.
mid.air

AMY MATHERS
P8–9
www.paperamy.co.uk

SARA LOUISE MATTHEWS
P90–91
www.sarahlouisematthews.
com

MOLLY MCGRATH
P100–101
www.mollymdesigns.com

JUSTYNA MEDOŃ,
ADDICTED TO PATTERNS
P66–67
www.justynamedon.uk

SIMONA MEESAIYATI
P146–147
www.instagram.com/simona.
paperart

CARLOS MEIRA
P76–77
www.carlosmeira.com

HANNAH MILES PAPERART
P94–95
hannahmilespaperart.com

GEORGIE MONICA
P86–87
www.georgiemonica.com

HATTIE NEWMAN
P126–127
www.hattienewman.co.uk

HANNAH NUNN
P20–21
www.hannahnunn.co.uk

EIKO OJALA
P74–75
www.ploom.tv

OLLANSKI
P42–43
www.ollanski.com

PAOLA PARONETTO
P134–135
www.paola-paronetto.com

CLARE PENTLOW
P80–81
www.cjpdesigns.co.uk

SAM PIERPOINT
P52–53
www.sampierpoint.com

SAMANTHA QUINN
P54–55
www.squinnandco.co.uk

SOPHIE RAE
P150–151
www.sophie-rae.com

LAURA REED DESIGN
P24–25
www.laurareeddesign.co.uk

LUCHA RODRÍGUEZ
P124–125
www.love-lucha-now.org

RAYA SADER BUJANA
P138–139
www.raya.studio

LAURA SAYERS
P106–107
www.lauraksayers.com

MARC SCHWEIZER
P38–39
www.schweizerpapierschnitt.ch

FREYA SCOTT
P88–89
www.paperwilds.co.uk

OLGA SKOROKHOD
P164–165
www.instagram.com/
olgaladyart

GABRIELA STUDER
P18–19
www.gabystuder.com

FIDELI SUNDQVIST
P84–85
www.fidelisundqvist.com

EMANUELE TARCHINI
P82–83
www.leledillipaperart.com

TIM VAN EENENNAAM
P156–157
www.timvaneenennaam.nl

VERA VAN WOLFEREN
P158–159
www.veravanwolferen.nl

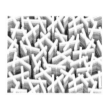

MAUD VANTOURS
P36–37
www.maudvantours.com

HAGAR VARDIMON
P98–99
www.hagarvardimon.com

KATHARINE WATSON
P116–117
www.kwatson.com

GORDY WRIGHT
P96–97
www.gordywright.com

STEPHANIE WUNDERLICH
P56–57
www.wunderlich-illustration.
de

ROSA YOO
P50–51
www.instagram.com/
rosaiyoo

BARI ZAKI
P70–71
www.barizaki.com

EUGENIA ZOLOTO
P78–79
www.instagram.com/
eugenia_zoloto